INFLATION - WHAT IT IS, WHAT IT ISN'T, AND WHO'S RESPONSIBLE FOR IT

Kelsey Williams

INFLATION - WHAT IT IS, WHAT IT ISN'T, AND WHO'S RESPONSIBLE FOR IT
Copyright © 2018 by Kelsey Williams

All rights reserved. No part of this book may be reproduced or transmitted in any form or by any means without written permission from the author.

ISBN 9781976986284

Printed in USA

Introduction

Inflation is an insidious threat to our financial and economic security. It has been foisted upon us to the point that we are in danger of losing much more than the value of our money. The capital markets are facing risks of immensely greater proportion than those of 2008-09. Economic activity is primarily financed by credit and we are hooked on the drug of money and higher prices - for everything. We are told often that inflation is spontaneous and that we must learn to mange its effects. That is not true. Inflation is intentional and practiced by governments and central banks the world over. And its effects are unpredictable and destructive. In addition, the effects of inflation are cumulative; hence, they tend to be more volatile, ongoing. And buried underneath all of the surface weaknesses is the specter of fractional-reserve banking. It is the legalized version of Ponzi scheme. A special section on the topic is included.

Inflation Is Caused By Government

Inflation is the debasement of money by the government.

It is not an increase in the general level of prices for goods and services.

The above statements are critical to an understanding and correct interpretation of events which are happening today that are casually attributable to inflation.

There is only one cause of inflation: government. The term government also includes central banks; especially the U.S. Federal Reserve Bank.

Inflation is not caused by greedy businesses, excessive wage demands, or accelerated consumer spending. Even government's own propensity to spend, as reckless as it is, does not cause inflation. And that does not contradict the statement that government is the only cause of inflation. They are - but not because of their spending habits.

Economic growth does not lead to higher inflation. There are statements made often that imply a link between growth in our economy and inflation. It is said that we have to "manage the growth" so the economy doesn't "grow too quickly" and "trigger higher inflation". These statements are false and misleading.

Also, inflation will not "accelerate…due to higher energy prices and stronger wage growth that leads firms to raise prices". It is possible - even likely - that inflation will accelerate over the next couple of years, but it won't/can't be for the reasons stated.

So how does the government cause inflation? Time for a bit of history...

Early ruling monarchs would 'clip' small pieces of the coins they accumulated through taxes and other levies against their subjects. The clipped pieces were melted down and fabricated into new coins. All of the coins were then returned to circulation. And all were assumed to be equal in value.

As the process evolved, and more and more clipped coins showed up in circulation, people became more outwardly suspicious and concerned. Thus, the ruling powers began altering/reducing the precious metal content of the coins. This lowered the cost to fabricate and issue new coins. No need to clip the coins anymore.

From the above example it is not hard to see how almost anything used as money could be altered in some way to satisfy the whims of government. But a process such as this was cumbersome and inconvenient. There had to be a better way. And there was.

Enter: Paper Money

With the advent of the printing press (moveable type) and continued improvements to the mechanics of replicating words and numbers in an easily recognizable fashion, paper money was now in vogue - big time.

However, people viewed the new 'money' with healthy skepticism. Coins with precious metal content continued to circulate alongside the new paper money. Hence, it was necessary, at least initially, for government to maintain a link of some kind between money of known value vs. money of no value in order to encourage its use.

Over time that link was severed; partially at first, then completely. And it was done by fiat (a decree or order of government).

Not only does our money today have no intrinsic value, it is inflated (and therefore debased) continuously and ongoing through subtle and more sophisticated ways such as fractional-reserve banking and expansion of credit. The printing press is still at the core and is humming 24/7 but the digital age has ushered in new and ingenious ways to fool the people.

Government causes inflation by expanding the supply of money and credit. And that expansion of the money supply cheapens the value of all the money. Which is why, over time, the US dollar continues to lose value. It takes more dollars today to purchase what could have been purchased ten years ago, twenty years ago, etc. And it has been going on for over one hundred years. (More specifically, our current inflation problems correlate with the origin of the U.S. Federal Reserve Bank.)

What most people refer to as inflation or its causes are neither. They are the effects of inflation. The increase in the general level of prices for goods and services is the result of inflation that was already created - the expansion of the supply of money and credit by government.

The Federal Reserve Bank of the United States was established in 1913. At that time the U.S. dollar was fully convertible into gold at a rate of twenty ($20.67) dollars per ounce. You could exchange paper currency of twenty dollars for one ounce of gold in coin form; and vice-versa. The coins were minted by the U.S. government. Gold in other forms (dust, flakes, nuggets, etc) also had circulated as money at the same ratio of twenty dollars to the ounce once its purity and weight was established.

In 1933 President Roosevelt issued an executive order "forbidding the hoarding of gold coin, gold bullion, and gold certificates within the continental United States". U.S. paper currency would no longer be convertible into gold for U.S. citizens but foreign holders (primarily foreign governments) could continue to redeem their holdings of U.S. dollars for gold at the "new, official" rate of $35.00 to the ounce. But what does that really mean?

If you were a foreign holder of U.S. dollars, you had just been told that your stash of 'money' (in the form of U.S. currency) was now worth forty-one percent less than previously. It was a tacit admission by the U.S. government that they had been 'inflating' the money supply aggressively as evidenced by the cumulative effects of that inflation showing up in the cost of goods and services (i.e. average cost of loaf of bread/gallon of gasoline).

The Depression (1930s) and World War II (1940s) conveniently received much of the blame. But things progressed reasonably well throughout the fifties and sixties.

By the late 1960s and early 1970s foreign governments were demanding returns of their gold on deposit here in the U.S. Some of that gold was the result of new redemptions of the accumulation of U.S. dollars which they held and which were guaranteed by the U.S. government as redeemable in gold.

In 1964, the United States ended its use of silver in the minting of coins used for legal tender. And, in 1971, President Nixon suspended convertibility of the U.S. dollar into gold by foreign nations.

For the past forty-six years there has been no convertibility of U.S. dollars (i.e. paper) into gold (i.e. real money). The U.S. dollar is money because the government says it is.

Fractional-Reserve Banking

If there is any one thing in particular that threatens the collapse of our banking system and financial structures worldwide, it is the practice of fractional-reserve banking. The subject is rarely mentioned in the financial press. When it is mentioned, a clear explanation is usually not available.

Here is an an excerpt from the article titled 'History Of Gold As Money'...

> The first gold coins appeared around 560 B.C. Over time it became a practice to store larger amounts of gold bullion in warehouses. Paper receipts were issued certifying that the gold was on deposit. These receipts were negotiable instruments of trade and commerce which could be signed over to others. They were not actual currency but are a presumed forerunner to our modern checking system.
>
> The warehouse proprietors ('bankers') decided they needed to find a way to increase their profits. Earning fees from their depository and safekeeping services wasn't enough. Since most of the gold remained in storage and most transactions involved exchange or transfer of paper receipts for the gold on deposit, they decided to issue 'loans' of the gold/money to others and charge interest. The cumulative amounts of gold loaned out could not exceed the amount of gold held in storage. And, hopefully, not too many depositors would ask to redeem their physical gold at the same time.
>
> It seemed to be a workable system. But apparently the 'bankers' were not content. They soon started issuing more loans/receipts for gold which did not exist. Of course they saw no need to inform anyone of their actions and the receipts still stated that they were redeemable in fixed amounts of gold. And when someone wanted to take possession of their gold on a physical basis they could still do so. Up to a point.

Fractional-reserve accounting by warehouses/banks was the original starting point for the credit expansion that now engulfs our world economy.

Here is an example of how this works today...

Your brother-in-law pays you thirty thousand dollars he borrowed three years ago. You decide to put the money in a time deposit (one year CD, etc.) at your bank. At the end of the day when your banker balances his books he finds that deposits at the bank exceed the funds which are currently loaned out/invested by an amount in excess of the ten percent US Federal Reserve requirement. And since that surplus amount is now available for new loans and additional investments, your bank's loan committee and investment department are busily engaged in efforts to allocate those funds on a - hopefully - profitable basis. After due consideration, it loans twelve thousand dollars to Jane, who wants to buy a car and fifteen thousand dollars to a local entrepreneur.

Jane pays the twelve thousand dollars to Mr. Smith who is selling the car to her (private transaction). She then drives away in her new car and Mr. Smith deposits the money in his bank which subsequently loans out ten thousand eight hundred dollars to a local dentist who is expanding his practice.

The local entrepreneur deposits the fifteen thousand dollars in his business account which is at the same bank that loaned him the money. Voila! The same bank which made the two loans now has fifteen thousand dollars in 'new' deposits of which it can lend out or invest another thirteen thousand five dollars. Which it promptly does.

The original deposit of thirty thousand dollars has grown to $81,300! How? By lending and investing a majority of the same money over and over again.

US Federal Reserve regulations require banks to keep on deposit an amount of money equal to ten percent of the deposits they take in (checking, savings, CDs, etc.). The remaining ninety percent can be loaned out or invested. (There are exceptions, allowances, and variations to the requirements depending on deposit type, amount, etc. There are also ways to meet the requirement other than just holding cash reserves.)

And that is just the tip of the iceberg. Once the money from each successive transaction is deposited, the process continues to repeat itself ad infinitum, continually adding to the total amount of dollars in the system.

Historically, early on, convertibility (exchangeable for physical gold) of warehouse receipts - and then paper currency - was maintained. This provided a restraint on the limits to which bankers could go in expanding the practice of fractional-reserve banking.

As late as the early twentieth century, U.S. paper currency was issued with a clear statement specifying that it was redeemable for specific amounts of gold at fixed rates. In addition, gold circulated concurrently with U.S. paper currency and the two were interchangeable.

Questions arose as to the value of the paper currency. And more and more individuals, companies, and countries opted for real money - gold. There simply wasn't enough gold to meet the redemption demands. And to whatever extent it was available, the banks and the government didn't want to release it.

President Nixon's suspension of U.S dollar convertibility (into gold) in 1971 freed the government of any final restraints or pretenses which could interfere with their dollar creation efforts. The Fed obliged by continuing to generously expand the supply of money and credit. Once additional money was made available, fractional-reserve banking kicked in.

Fractional-reserve banking is ongoing. It is at the core of the Federal Reserve's efforts to expand the supply of money and credit. Hence, the number of U.S. dollars continues to increase and their value continues to erode. Their value at any given time is always suspect. How can we possibly know what a dollar is worth when there is an unlimited supply and no constancy?

Noted and respected fund manager, Bill Gross said:

"It still mystifies me how a banking system can create money out of thin air, but it does. By rough estimates, banks and their shadows have turned $3 trillion of "base" credit into $65 trillion + of "unreserved" credit in the United States alone..."

What is truly amazing is the extent to which our banking system can hold itself together. And, to whatever extent the Fed's efforts have kept the system from imploding, it is noteworthy that we look to and depend on the perpetrator of the crime to rescue us. Even worse, the solution(s) offered are the very same actions that led to the current predicament. Spend more and borrow more.

So what is the danger? Does over-leveraged use of money really pose significant risks to the viability of our monetary system?

Bob has ten thousand dollars that he doesn't know what to do with so he gives it to his best friend, Sam, for safekeeping. Bob tells Sam that he does not expect to need the money anytime soon, but he may want to get some of it from time to time. And, of course, if the unexpected happens (it always does) he may need to have access to more - or all - of it.

Since Sam is a specialist in financial matters and has considerable investment expertise he decides to invest four thousand dollars of Bob's money in US Treasury notes. Sam also loans five thousand dollars to a friend of his who is a homebuilder. Sam will earn interest on the construction loan in addition to a modest return on the US Treasury notes he purchased. Not bad. Especially since he does not have to pay Bob more than a pittance for 'watching' his money for him. Maybe Bob should pay Sam something for the good job he is doing (think negative interest rates).

Sam has decided to keep one thousand dollars of Bob's money available in case it is needed. Good thing, too. After one week, Bob asks Sam for one thousand dollars of his money back in order to take care of some unexpected expenses. Sam promptly pays Bob his one thousand dollars.

Sam now feels that the likelihood of Bob needing more of his money anytime soon is a remote possibility. Hence, he pledges the US Treasury notes as collateral and borrows four thousand dollars. He keeps one thousand in cash and loans another three thousand dollars to his friend, the home builder.

Bob sees the success the builder and others are having and decides that he wants to invest his remaining nine thousand dollars in real estate. So he goes to see Sam.

Sam only has one thousand dollars of Bob's money available and gives it to him right away. He tells Bob that he will have the rest of his money shortly.

Sam calls his builder friend right away. The builder tells Sam that a couple his homes have not sold yet and the money to repay Sam isn't available until the homes are sold.

Sam could sell the four thousand dollars in US Treasury Notes in order to access part of the money needed to pay Bob. But the proceeds would have to be used first to pay off the loan for which they are pledged as collateral. Since the loan amount is nearly identical to the market value of the US Treasury notes, no additional funds would be available.

Bob, meanwhile, decides that he won't start investing in real estate as he had planned. Therefore, he won't need the rest of his money right now.

Except that when his wife gets home from work, he learns that one of their kids needs braces on her teeth. Also, the interest rate reset on their home mortgage has taken effect triggering a substantial increase in their mortgage payment. He decides that he might need to draw from his money (that Sam has charge of) after all.

When he calls on Sam the next day, Bob is shocked to find out that his money is not available. And Sam doesn't know when it will be available.

The above story is imaginary, incomplete, and unending. But it is illustrative of the risks of fractional-reserve banking. The amounts are small and the scenario simple for the sake of clarity. If too many 'Bob's' want their money at one time or can't make their mortgage payments....

Now consider the implications of adding trillions of dollars of esoteric financial products to the mix. Things like collateralized debt obligations, leveraged ETFs, options on futures, etc. And those things are in addition to ordinary securities margin accounts.

It can be argued that the use of funds made available by banks via fractional-reserve accounting is productive and helpful. Nevertheless, that does not reduce the risk to the system. It adds to it. Because it furthers leverages the same dollars over and over again. And many of the uses are risky enough on their own.

The monetary value we place on anything of consequence is underpinned by an extension of credit. That credit starts with fractional-reserve banking. This leads to credit cards, student loans, auto loans, construction loans, mortgages, etc.

Fractional-reserve banking is the foundation for the 'inverted' debt pyramid that threatens the collapse of our financial system.

The Effects Of Inflation

The Arab Oil Embargo in 1973 and the demands for more money for oil which led to the formation of the Organization Of Petroleum Exporting Countries (OPEC) followed close behind President Nixon's severance of all ties of the US dollar to gold. The underlying fact of the matter was that the dollars which they were receiving for their oil were worth less (not quite 'worthless') and had been losing value for several decades. And the price had been fixed for decades.

To understand this better, imagine that you were a company selling widgets for $1 each. According to your contract you cannot receive any more than that. Fast forward twenty or thirty years. You are still selling lots of widgets and still receiving $1 for each one you sell. But your costs over the years have continued to climb. And it also costs you more for everything you buy to maintain your standard of living. And it's not just you. Everyone is paying more for everything. Yet, on an ongoing, year-to-year basis, things seem reasonably normal. But prices now are rising more frequently and the rate of increase is higher than before. What is going on?

The effects of inflation are showing up. Those effects can be very subtle at first, or not noticed at all. But at some point in time the cumulative effects of inflation become more obvious and everyone starts acting differently. Businesses try to plan for it and individuals invest with inflation in mind. If your dollars were freely convertible into equivalent amounts of gold based on the prices in effect at the time of your original contract to produce widgets - or sell barrels of oil - then you could just exchange your dollars for gold. Which is exactly what happened.

Foreign governments in the late sixties began to demand the gold to which they were legally entitled. And countries which produced and sold oil wanted a higher price for their oil.

As people became more aware of the effects of inflation they started looking for reasons. And for guilty parties. Government was quick to act of course. They started by implementing wage and price controls. This is like setting the stove burner on 'high' and putting a lid on the pot with no release for the pressure. And they talk a lot.

They have talked enough over the past thirty years to frighten us into thinking that our own spending and saving habits are the problem. Sometimes the blame is directed at foreign countries and their currencies -China/Yuan for example.

Our sense of unfairness over China's attempts to weaken the Yuan seem to be misplaced. We criticize them for doing the same things the US government and Federal Reserve have been doing for over one hundred years.

The inflation (expansion of the supply of money and credit) produced by the Federal Reserve is deliberate and intentional. And ongoing. The effects of that inflation are volatile and unpredictable.

During the seventies, prices for basic necessities were rising on a weekly, even daily, basis. But things eventually settled down and we had an extended period of stability and relative US dollar strength for a couple of decades.

Even with the hugely, inflationary response of the Federal Reserve in 2008 and afterwards we did not see the "obvious substantial increase in the general level of prices for goods and services" that some expected and predicted. But we did see a resurgence of higher prices for financial assets like stocks and real estate.

And yet, the effects of inflation are very clear. How much are you paying for things today compared to a few years ago? ten years ago? twenty or thirty?

As time marches on, the effects of government inflation will become more extreme and more unpredictable. And, over time, the U.S dollar will continue to decline in value.

*****

The average cost for a loaf of bread in 1930 was ten cents ($.10). The average cost for a gallon of gasoline was also ten cents. With gold priced in U.S. dollars at $20.00 per ounce, you could at that time purchase two hundred loaves of bread or two hundred gallons of gasoline (or some combination thereof).

Twenty dollars of paper currency OR one ounce of gold were equal in purchasing power. The gold equivalent was usually in the form of a coin called a Double Eagle. It contained .968 ounce of gold, which, at the official gold price of $20.67 per ounce, equals $20.00.

Over the next four decades the cost for a loaf of bread/gallon of gasoline continued to increase such that in 1970 the respective costs were twenty-five cents/thirty-six cents. An ounce of gold (at $40.00) would purchase one hundred sixty loaves of bread/one hundred eleven gallons of gasoline. That is considerably less than the two hundred units of either item which could have been purchased in 1930.

But the numbers are even worse when we look at what twenty dollars of U.S. paper currency would buy in 1970: eighty loaves of bread/fifty-five gallons of gasoline. Both gold and the U.S. dollar lost purchasing power over the forty-year period 1930-70 but the U.S. dollar was the "biggest loser".

In 1968, the United States Government again revalued gold officially at $40.00 per ounce and at the same time acknowledged a free market for gold which could operate on its own, independently. However, the U.S. would not recognize the free market price in any official dealings or transactions.

By 1971 things were getting a bit dicey. Foreign governments wanted their gold, but the U.S. did not want to release it. Or, they didn't have it. Probably some combination of both. So, in August 1971, President Nixon suspended any further convertibility of U.S. dollars into gold by non-U.S. citizens. All hell broke loose. Literally.

Prices of goods and services in the United States began rising rapidly and the U.S. dollar price of gold peaked in 1980 at $850.00 per ounce. The average price for gold in 1980 was $615.00 per ounce.

And, by 1980 the average cost of a loaf of bread was $.50 (double what it was in 1970) and the average cost of a gallon of gasoline had settled out at $1.19. The above stated average U.S. dollar price of gold ($615.00 per ounce) would purchase twelve hundred thirty loaves of bread or five hundred sixteen gallons of gasoline. And the good old U.S. dollar? Twenty dollars in U.S. paper currency would buy forty loaves of bread/ seventeen gallons of gasoline.

Ten years later, in 1990, a loaf of bread had increased to $.70 and a gallon of gasoline was up to $1.34. With gold at $338.00 per ounce you could purchase four hundred eighty-two loaves of bread/two hundred fifty-two gallons of gasoline. Twenty U.S. dollars would buy twenty-eight loaves of bread/fifteen gallons of gasoline.

Even though the average price of gold dropped (reflecting a period of relative U.S. dollar strength) by forty-five percent in the ten-year period from 1980-1990, you could still buy more bread or gasoline than you could sixty years earlier.

So where are we today? The average cost of a loaf of bread and a gallon of gasoline are approximately the same - about $2.50. With gold at $1300.00 per ounce you can purchase five hundred twenty loaves of bread or five hundred twenty gallons of gasoline which is nearly one hundred sixty percent MORE than the amount you could have purchased with one ounce of gold in 1930.

And twenty dollars in U.S. currency will purchase eight loaves of bread or eight gallons of gasoline which is ninety-six percent LESS than the amount you could have purchased with twenty dollars of U.S. currency in 1930.

Mansa Musa

From Wikipedia...

Musa Keita I (c. 1280 - c. 1337) was the tenth Mansa, which translates as "sultan" (king) or "emperor", of the wealthy West African Mali Empire.

During his reign Mali may have been the largest producer of gold in the world at a point of exceptional demand. One of the richest people in history, he is known to have been enormously wealthy; reported as being inconceivably rich by contemporaries, "There's really no way to put an accurate number on his wealth" (Davidson 2015).

Musa made his pilgrimage (to Mecca) between 1324 - 1325. His procession reportedly included 60,000 men, including 12,000 slaves who each carried 4 lb (1.8 kg) of gold bars and heralds dressed in silks who bore gold staffs, organized horses, and handled bags. Musa provided all necessities for the procession, feeding the entire company of men and animals. Those animals included 80 camels which each carried 50-300 lb (23-136 kg) of gold dust. Musa gave the gold to the poor he met along his route. Musa not only gave to the cities he passed on the way to Mecca, including Cairo and Medina, but also traded gold for souvenirs. It was reported that he built a mosque every Friday.

But Musa's generous actions inadvertently devastated the economy of the regions through which he passed. In the cities of Cairo, Medina, and Mecca, the sudden influx of gold devalued the metal for the next decade. Prices on goods and wares greatly inflated. To rectify the gold market, on his way back from Mecca, Musa borrowed all the gold he could carry from money-lenders in Cairo, at high interest. This is the only time recorded in history that one man directly controlled the price of gold in the Mediterranean.

Some historians consider Musa to be the single, most wealthy individual in history and his wealth is estimated to be the inflation-adjusted equivalent of four hundred billion US dollars in today's money.

Musa's actions were charitable and laudable. And the effects of his actions on the gold market at the time were unintentional. Yet, still inevitable.

The "sudden influx of gold" constituted an increase in the supply of money which resulted in "prices on goods and wares greatly inflated". This is a classic, historical example of inflation.

The economies of the regions that Musa visited were relatively industrious with a reasonably stable economy. And the gold which Musa carried with him was not, for the most part, circulating as part of the money supply in the world at that time. In a short period of time, large amounts of gold (i.e. money) were put in circulation. With more money available, more aggressive bidding for various "goods and wares" drove prices for those items higher.

The 'higher prices' for goods and wares was an inverse reflection of the loss of purchasing power of the money (gold) in circulation.

Gold is not immune to inflation. This is not an indictment of gold. But it does serve to illustrate the vulnerability of money regarding the consequences of inflation. And Mansa Musa acted benevolently, as an individual. Also, his actions and resulting effects were basically a one-time event.

On the other hand, inflation, as practiced by the United States Government and the Federal Reserve, is intentional and perpetual. Over one hundred years old and still going strong. The effects of those efforts are unpredictable and wildly volatile. And the value of our money continues to erode.

And, whereas, Musa acted immediately to help alleviate the problem which his actions created by borrowing "all the gold he could carry from money-lenders in Cairo, at high interest", the Federal Reserve inflicts harm on the monetary system by continually expanding the supply of money and credit. It will distort every monetary measure of value we are inclined to rely on and at some point the system will implode.

The problems arising from Musa's actions were systemic and not related to the 'form' of money in use. And those problems were limited because the money supply was limited. No one could produce more money (i.e. gold) by printing it.

Which is why governments hate gold. It is a restraint on their free-spending, expansionary policies. Even the example of Mansa Musa does not diminish the role gold plays in this regard. Or its rightful place as real money - original money.

Summary

The United States Government, via the Federal Reserve Bank, has been practicing inflation regularly for over one hundred years. They are good at it. Their efforts have resulted in a ninety-eight percent reduction in the purchasing power of the U.S. dollar.

The Fed has the tools to expand and contract the money supply. But on a continuous basis, and ongoing since its inception, the focus is on expansion.

The continued, ever-increasing expansion of money and credit destroys the value of existing money. Over time, as the existing money loses its value/purchasing power, the effects show up generally in the form of rising prices.

This is why it costs more today to buy life's necessities (and luxuries) than it did ten or twenty years ago. On a year-to-year basis it is usually not too noticeable. But sometimes the symptoms are exacerbated such as in the seventies.

Government causes inflation and pursues it for its own selfish reasons. A government does not voluntarily stop inflating its currency. Hence, the U.S. dollar and our financial system bear increasing risk.

As we become more dependent on the inflation to keep things going, the effects of each successive expansionary effort have less impact. And we become more vulnerable in two ways.

The first is an overdose. Too much money, too quickly, leads to complete destruction and repudiation - death - of the currency. The runaway or hyper-inflation in Germany in the 1920s is a defining example.

The second is a credit collapse. Not enough money at the right time and the economy - just like a drug addict - slips into withdrawal. And the effects of withdrawal (monetarily speaking) could be so bad as to usher in true deflation and a full-scale depression.

Just as a drug addict must endure pain and discomfort in order to cleanse himself, so must it be with our monetary system. The dilemma results from the cumulative effects of repeated bad choices over long periods of time.

What's worse, however, is the increased likelihood that the entire system will collapse under its own weight, no matter how hard the Federal Reserve and the government try to avoid the inevitable consequences.

Something similar to 2008-09 is going to occur again. Only it will be much worse. And regardless of the traditional, reactionary talk and efforts to save us, the system will likely not withstand the "symptoms of withdrawal".

Kelsey Williams is a gold analyst and writer. His website, Kelsey's Gold Facts at kelseywilliamsgold.com contains self-authored articles written for the purpose of educating and informing others about gold within an historical context. In addition to gold, he writes about inflation, interest rates and the Federal Reserve. His articles are published on various international websites. He has more than forty years experience in the financial services industry including fourteen years as a full-service financial planner. During the 1970s he advised clients regarding the purchase of gold and silver and continued to do so throughout his career.